WITHDRAWN

D0593621

BECCA·CAHAN

Published by Sellers Publishing, Inc.

Copyright © 2018 Sellers Publishing, Inc.
Illustrations © 2018 Becca Cahan
All rights reserved.

Sellers Publishing, Inc.
161 John Roberts Road, South Portland, Maine 04106
Visit our website: www.sellerspublishing.com • E-mail: rsp@rsvp.com

Mary L. Baldwin, Managing Editor
Charlotte Cromwell, Production Editor

ISBN 13: 978-1-4162-4666-4

10 9 8 7 6 5 4 3 2 1

Printed in China.

‹ SHE › PERSISTED

QUOTES to MOTIVATE+INSPIRE

art by
BECCA♥CAHAN

SELLERS
PUBLISHING

MAYA ANGELOU was an award-winning author, poet, civil rights activist, and recipient of the Presidential Medal of Freedom. She wrote the words, "I'm a woman, phenomenally. Phenomenal woman, that's me."
Her advice to young women of the world: Develop courage.

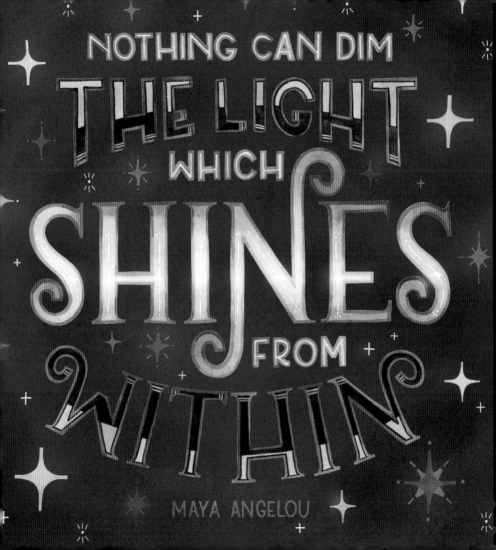

it takes

COURAGE

TO grow UP
&
BECOME WHO YOU
really are

e.e. cummings

Bravery:

noun · BRAV·ER·Y \'brav(ə)rē/

courageous behavior
or character

Strength grows in the
moments when you think
you can't go on but you
keep going anyway.

~ Former first lady ~

MICHELLE OBAMA is a strong
advocate for women's rights and believes that
a country can never truly flourish if it stifles the
potential of its women and deprives itself of the
contributions of half of its citizens.

MOMENTUM:

noun · MO·MEN·TUM /mō'men(t)əm/

driving force gained by the
development of a process
or course of events

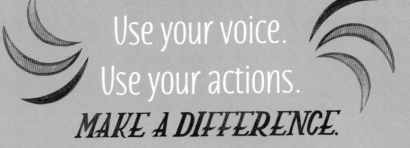

Use your voice.
Use your actions.
MAKE A DIFFERENCE.

As a young girl, MALALA YOUSAFZAI defied the Taliban in Pakistan by demanding that all girls be allowed to receive an education. Against injury and extreme adverstiy, she went on to receive the Nobel Peace Prize in 2014.

I am STRONGER than FEAR

Malala Yousafzai

DIGNITY:

noun · DIG·NI·TY /dignədē/
a sense of pride in oneself; self-respect

If you **AIM** at nothing
you won't hit **ANYTHING**.

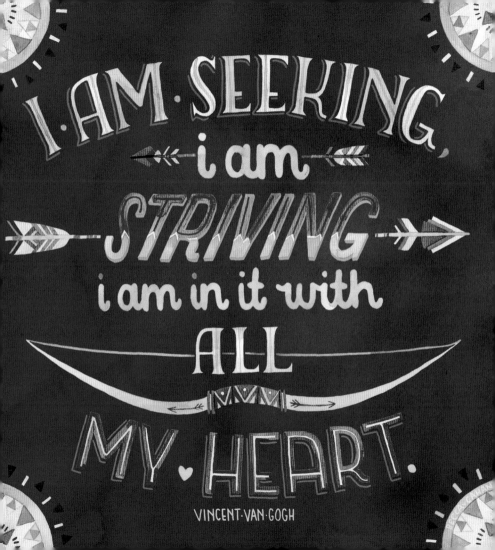

J.K. Rowling is a British novelist, screenwriter, and producer. In the face of adversity, she went from being a poor, single mother with no job, to writing one of the most popular and successful fantasy series of all times. Rowling credits her imagination, determination, and ability to survive for emerging from her setbacks stronger and wiser.

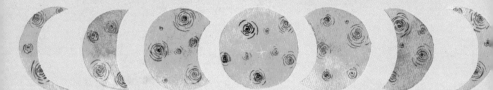

CREATIVITY:
noun · CRE·A·TIV·I·TY /krēāˈtivədē
the ability to form new ideas or concepts

THE SECRET TO GETTING AHEAD IS GETTING STARTED

AGATHA CHRISTIE

Eleanor Roosevelt was the longest-serving First Lady throughout her husband's four terms as the 32nd president of the United States. Breaking White House precedence, she gave lectures, held press conferences, and openly expressed her opinions. As an activist for the underprivileged of all races and religions, she played a major role in the drafting and adoption of the Universal Declaration of Human Rights.

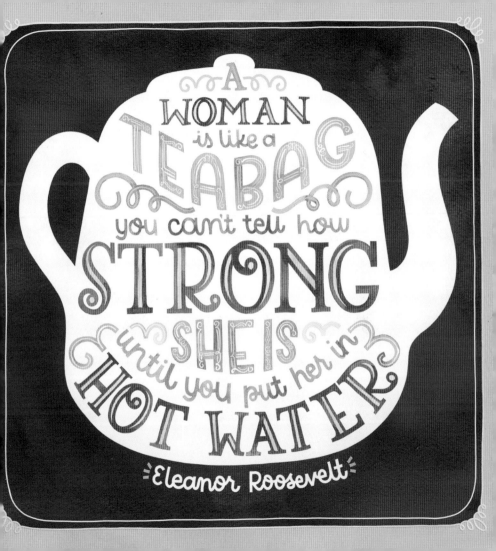

Intention:

noun · in·ten·tion \ in'ten(t)SH(ə)n \
purpose, deliberateness, a process, a plan

Life is the greatest
challenge there is.
Rise up, meet it, and
become stronger.

Acting under divine
guidance, JOAN OF ARC,
a determined 19-year-
old peasant girl led
the French army to
victory over the English.
A military leader,
and martyr, she was
canonized as a
saint in 1920.

PERSISTENCE:

noun • PER·SIST·ENCE \pər'sistəns\

steadfast; firm course of action despite opposition

WE MAY ENCOUNTER MANY DEFEATS, BUT WE MAY NOT BE DEFEATED

—MAYA·ANGELOU—

Don't let circumstances
define you. Push the
boundaries and always
be true to yourself.

Oprah Winfrey became the first African American female to host a nationally syndicated daily talk show in 1986.
She is a dedicated activist for children's rights, a staunch advocate for female education, and supports various charitable projects that help improve the quality of life for women around the world.

She believed SHE COULD, so SHE DID.

R.S. Grey, Scoring Wilder

confidence:

noun · CON·FI·DENCE \kanfədəns\

a feeling of self-assurance arising
from one's appreciation of one's
own abilities or qualities

Never settle.
Never give up.
Never stop believing in yourself.
YOU are WORTH it.

You must never be fearful about what you are doing when it is right.

ROSA PARKS

ROSA PARKS, an African American woman whose refusal to give up her seat on a bus to a white man, ignited the U.S. Civil Rights movement in 1955. She believed that differences of race, nationality, or religion should not be used to deny any human being citizenship rights or privileges.

Determination:

noun · DE·TER·MI·NA·TION /de,terme'naSH(ə)n/
firmness of purpose, resoluteness

Step outside your
comfort zone and accept
life's challenges.
Only then will you grow.

At an early age, COCO CHANEL experienced poverty, the death of her mother, and the abandonment of her father. Using her resourcefulness, she launched a global fashion empire that dominated the haute couture scene for decades.

BEAUTY BEGINS *the* MOMENT YOU DECIDE *to be* YOURSELF

Coco Chanel

SELF♥LOVE:

noun · SELF·LOVE \self'ləv/

regard for one's own well-being and happiness

TODAY
is the day
that will
change your life.

Prompted by her father's inability to read,
Grammy Award-winning country singer
DOLLY PARTON created a book-gifting program
to fight illiteracy. IMAGINATION LIBRARY
is a world-wide charity that provides
free books to young children.

PASSION:

noun · PAS·SION /paSHeN/
strong and barely
controllable emotion

Be the person who

INSPIRES
OTHERS

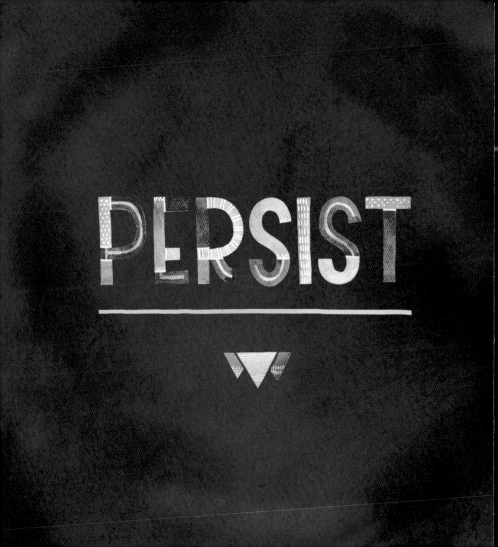